Recycle

KT-419-815

Kay Barnham

C153648383

**KENT
LIBRARIES & ARCHIVES**

C153648383

First published in Great Britain in 2006 by
Wayland, an imprint of Hachette Children's Books

Reprinted in 2007

This paperback edition published in 2008

Copyright © Wayland 2006

All rights reserved.

Wayland
338 Euston Road, London NW1 3BH

Wayland Australia
Level 17/207 Kent Street
Sydney, NSW 2000

Editor: Penny Worms
Senior Design Manager: Rosamund Saunders
Designer: Ben Ruocco, Tall Tree Ltd

British Library Cataloguing in Publication Data
Barnham, Kay
    Recycling. - (Environment action)
    1. Recycling (waste, etc.) - Juvenile literature
    I. Title
    363.7'282

ISBN 13: 978 0 7502 5509 7

Printed in China

Wayland is a division of Hachette Children's Books,
an Hachette Livre UK Company.
www.hachettelivre.co.uk

The publishers would like to thank the following for allowing us to
reproduce their pictures in this book:
Alamy: 16 (Daphne Christelis), 17 (Tina Manley), 21 (Neil Setchfield), 25
(Simon de Trey-White), 29 (Jim West). Corbis images: 6 (Chris Lisle), 20
(Alain Nogues). Ecoscene: 7 (Wayne Lawler), 10 (John Wilkinson), 12
(John Wilkinson), 13 (Sally Morgan), 19 (Angela Hampton), 23 (Sally
Morgan), 24 (Nick Hawkes), 27 (Kevin King), 28 (Rosemary Greenwood).
Getty images: 15 (Michael Paul), 18 (Dennis O'Clair), 26 (Alistair Berg).
Photolibrary: cover and 14 (J-C & D Pratt). Rex Features: 9, (Roy Garner),
11 (Action Press). Wayland Picture Library: title page and 4, 5, 8, 22.

Contents

What is Recycling?

Recycling is when something is not thrown away after use but is used again. When old bottles and jars are recycled, they are **melted down** and made into new bottles and jars.

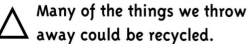 Many of the things we throw away could be recycled.

△ Lots of things can be recycled, such as cans, plastic bottles, cardboard, vegetable peelings and batteries.

Recycling is something that everyone can do – at home, at school and at work. Next time you think about putting something in the bin – stop! Look at it carefully. Is it something that could be recycled instead?

Why Recycle?

There are lots of reasons why we should recycle. It is often cheaper to recycle than it is to make brand-new things. Recycling is also a very good way of helping the **environment**, by saving natural materials, such as trees, oil and water.

△ Buying second-hand furniture is a good way of recycling. No new trees are needed.

We get wood from trees to make paper, furniture and buildings, and it can be burnt as **fuel**. But chopping down trees destroys animals' homes and causes damage to the area. It can even affect the weather and cause **floods**.

△ Almost three quarters of Indonesia's **rainforest** has been destroyed or cut down for our use.

Metal, glass and plastic are all made from natural materials.

Dealing with Rubbish

A lot of our rubbish is taken away and put into **landfills**, which are large holes dug into the earth. When a landfill is full, a layer of earth is spread over the top. It can take hundreds of years – and sometimes much longer – for the rubbish to rot away. Some rubbish never rots.

△ Rubbish trucks collect rubbish from outside our homes and shops.

Paper, garden **waste**, plastic, wood, metals, food and glass are all thrown away, but all of these things could be recycled. As landfills become full, we may run out of places to put our rubbish.

△ If we recycle things instead, we will not need so much space for rubbish.

FACT!

It is thought that disposable nappies take 500 years to break down. Cotton nappies can be re-used.

A Cleaner World

Pollution is dirty and unhealthy air or water. It can be caused when waste is burnt, buried or flushed away. Burning rubbish in **incinerators** turns it into **ash**, which is smaller and easier to deal with. But the fires can send harmful gases into the air.

△ Some experts think air pollution is causing **global warming**, making our world a hotter place.

△ Polluting rivers and streams harms wildlife, plants and trees.

When you flush the toilet or pull out a bath plug, the water flows to a **wastewater treatment works**. Here, the waste water is cleaned so that it can be used again. However, dirty water from **factories** often pours straight into rivers, streams and the sea.

Recycling Paper

Paper is made from wood **pulp**. Millions of valuable trees have been cut down to make paper. In some parts of the world, they are still being destroyed. Specially planted trees are now used to make most new paper. But recycled paper needs no new trees to make it!

△ You can use both sides of the paper or buy recycled paper for your letters and drawings.

Letters, newspapers, magazines, cardboard and **junk mail** are just some of the types of paper that can be recycled over and over again. Paper is mixed with water and mashed to a pulp. Next, it is cleaned. The pulp is then rolled thinly to make new paper.

△ This paper mill is making recycled paper.

FACT!

It takes much less **energy** and water to recycle paper than it does to make brand-new paper.

Recycling Glass

Every day, millions of glass bottles and jars are thrown away. But these could all be recycled. Glass is perfect for recycling. No matter how many times it is melted and reshaped, it will never become weaker.

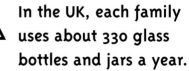 In the UK, each family uses about 330 glass bottles and jars a year.

△ Old glass jars can be re-used. Some people fill them with home-made jam.

When glass is recycled, the **temperature** of the **furnace** is cooler than it needs to be for making new glass. This saves energy and reduces pollution. It also means that fewer natural materials, such as sand and limestone, need to be used.

Recycling Cans

Food tins and drink cans are made from steel and aluminium. Both of these metals are easy and cheap to recycle. It takes a lot of energy to **mine** aluminium and then make it into cans, foil, trays, lids and chocolate wrappers. Recycling aluminium uses a tiny fraction of the energy needed to make new aluminium.

△ In the UK, people drink more than 5,000 million cans of drink a year. It is very important that they are recycled.

△ There is a huge range of tinned food at the supermarket. All these cans could be recycled.

Next time you visit the supermarket, look at the shelves of tins and cans – every single one will be made of some recycled material.

FACT!

Food sold in UK supermarkets is wrapped in 35,000 tonnes of aluminium. This is about the same weight as 2,500 double-decker buses!

Recycling Plastics

Plastic causes lots of problems for the environment. If thrown away, many types of plastic will never rot. If plastic is burnt, it produces poisonous smoke. Plastic is made from oil. Oil supplies will not last for ever.

Recycled plastic can be made into many things, including clothing! It takes 25 large plastic bottles to make one warm fleece.

Recycling plastic is expensive. The best thing to do with plastic is to use it again, instead of throwing it away. Plastic carrier bags can be used lots of times, or you can buy a strong reusable shopping bag at most supermarkets.

△ Take a sturdy bag with you when you go shopping. It lasts much longer and is stronger too!

FACT!

Recycled plastic can also be made into anoraks, sleeping bags, pipes, furniture, fences and even signposts!

Recycling Textiles

Textiles are clothes, sheets and pillowcases, curtains, carpets and even shoes. People often throw them away before they are worn out. Instead, it would be better to re-use or recycle them. Perhaps someone else could wear them. Also, textiles can be recycled to make clothes, furniture padding, paper and mattresses.

 Many charities clean and send second-hand clothes to people who need them.

△ Top fashion designers look for ideas in second-hand clothes shops. They are recycling designs!

Charity shops sell second-hand clothes to make money for lots of good causes. They are much cheaper than new clothes. You might be able to buy a whole outfit for the price of a new pair of socks!

Reduce, Re-use, Recycle!

There are three important ways we can cut down the rubbish that is buried in landfills or burnt in incinerators. We can **reduce**, re-use or recycle our waste.

If we reduce the amount of things we use, there is less to throw away. For example, when people send letters, they use pens, paper and envelopes. **Emails** require no materials at all!

◁ Junk modelling is a fantastic way of re-using cardboard tubes, yoghurt pots and many other sorts of junk.

△ If you check the labels, you can find many items made from recycled materials.

Instead of throwing old things away, we can re-use or recycle them. And finally, we can buy recycled things, such as recycled paper, kitchen roll and bin liners.

Recycling at Home

In lots of towns and cities, councils **collect** rubbish from homes. They collect material for recycling too. People fill up large plastic boxes and bags with newspaper, cardboard, bottles, cans and plastic. They put these out for collection.

 Ready meals have lots of packaging, but loose vegetables have none at all! Think how much packaging material could be saved if we didn't buy packaged food.

After birthdays or Christmas, think before you throw away wrapping paper, cards and cardboard. You could use it again or put it in the recycling box. Christmas trees with roots can be planted in the garden and then used the next year.

FACT!

In one year in the UK, there would be enough household rubbish to fill dustbins stretching all the way from the Earth to the Moon and back.

△ Christmas trees can also be chopped up into pieces. Gardeners can spread these onto their soil to help plants grow.

Recycling at School

You might already recycle paper at school, but did you know that there are many more ways of helping to reduce waste?

You can raise money for your school or a local charity, simply by recycling! Some businesses will pay for aluminium cans and foil. And the more you collect, the more money you will raise!

◁ Instead of drinking from a plastic bottle of water and then throwing the bottle away, why not refill it and use the bottle again?

Apple cores and other scraps of food can be rotted down to make **compost**. After some time, the compost is spread around flowers and bushes to feed them and make them grow big and strong.

Food scraps can be mixed with garden leaves to make a good compost.

More Ideas!

Instead of throwing away old toys and **trinkets**, why not have a garage sale or take them to a jumble sale? To you, your belongings might be old and dull. To someone else, they will be brand new and exciting!

△ You could sell your old toys at a boot fair and make some money.

△ Some charities collect old mobile phones, fix them and sell them on.

Charity shops don't just take old clothes and books. Did you know that some charities also recycle old mobile phones and computers, stamps and empty **printer cartridges**? Donating these things means that you can help charities to raise money and you are recycling, all at the same time!

Glossary

Ash – the grey powder left when something is burned

Collect – to gather things together

Compost – rotted vegetables and other waste that is added to soil as food for plants

Email – a message sent from one computer to another

Energy – the power needed to make things work

Environment – the world around us

Factories – buildings where people make things with machines

Floods – a lot of water covering land that is usually dry

Fuel – things that are burned to make energy

Furnace – a very hot oven, where things are melted

Global warming – when our planet becomes hotter

Incinerator – a very hot oven, where waste is burned

Junk mail – mail sent by companies to advertise their goods or services

Landfills – large holes dug into the earth where waste is buried

Melted down – changed from a solid into a liquid

Mine – to dig coal, metal or other natural materials out of the ground

Natural materials – things found on or in our planet that isn't made by people

Pollution – dirty or unhealthy air or water

Printer cartridge – an ink container that fits inside a printer

Pulp – a wet mushy mixture

Rainforest – a large forest in a hot part of the world

Recycling – when something is not thrown away after use but is used again

Reduce – to make something smaller or less

Re-use – to use something again

Temperature – how hot or cold something is

Textiles – anything made of fabric

Trinket – a piece of jewellery or an ornament

Waste – something that is not needed any more

Wastewater treatment works – a place where waste water is cleaned

Index